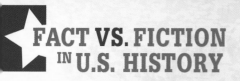

FACT VS. FICTION
IN U.S. HISTORY

ABNER
DOUBLEDAY

AND BASEBALL'S BEGINNING:
SEPARATING FACT FROM FICTION

by Nel Yomtov

CAPSTONE PRESS
a capstone imprint

Capstone Captivate is published by Capstone Press, an imprint of Capstone.
1710 Roe Crest Drive
North Mankato, Minnesota 56003
www.capstonepub.com

Library of Congress Cataloging-in-Publication Data is available on the Library of Congress website.
ISBN: 978-1-4966-9536-9 (library binding)
ISBN: 978-1-4966-9671-7 (paperback)
ISBN: 978-1-9771-5377-7 (eBook PDF)

Summary: Step up to the plate and separate fact from fiction in baseball's origins! Did Abner Doubleday really create America's favorite pastime, or does this story strike out? Learn all you can about baseball's beginnings.

Image Credits
Alamy: UtCon Collection, cover (bottom back), 8 (top); Getty Images: NY Daily News Archive/Seelig, 20, 24, Transcendental Graphics, 9, 21, UIG/Encyclopaedia Britannica, 11 (top); iStockphoto: wellglad, cover (bat), 11 (bottom); Library of Congress: cover (top right), 7 (top), 8 (bottom), 12, 18; The New York Public Library: 5 (right), 6 (left), 7 (bottom), 13, 15, 17, 19 (top); Newscom: Album/Oronoz, 25, Splash News/Derek Shook, 19 (bottom), UPI/ George Napolitano, 26; Shutterstock: Artur Didyk, cover (top left), Dan Thornberg, 5 (left), eurobanks, back cover, 6 (right), Joseph Sohm, 4, Keeton Gale, 28, Lunatictm, 10 (top), Morphart Creation, 27, Nagel Photography, 23, roibu, cover (ball), Witthaya lOvE, 10 (bottom)

Editorial Credits
Editor: Gena Chester; Designer: Kyle Grenz; Media Researcher: Svetlana Zhurkin; Production Specialist: Katy LaVigne

Source Notes
p. 16, "American Courage, Confidence . . ." America's National Game. New York: American Sports Publishing Company, 1911, p. 5.
p. 19, "Base Ball is too strenuous . . ." Ibid., p. 13.
p. 26, "I really believe that . . ." Tim Arango, "Myth of Baseball's Creation Endures, With a Prominent Fan" New York Times Online, https://www.nytimes.com/2010/11/13/sports/baseball/13doubleday.html
Accessed on May 20, 2020.

All internet sites appearing in back matter were available and accurate when this book was sent to press.

Printed and bound in the USA. PO#3837

Table of Contents

Words in **bold** are in the glossary.

Introduction

Baseball has been part of American life for more than 160 years. The sport is called America's pastime. The country's love of baseball has inspired books, movies, and songs. It has been a source of great joy and thrills for many American families.

A professional baseball game in Los Angeles, California

For more than 100 years, Americans have been told that a military man named Abner Doubleday invented the game of baseball. The story goes that Doubleday created baseball in the small, charming village of Cooperstown, New York. Most people believed the story. Many still do.

The story is not true: Abner Doubleday did not invent baseball. But the history of the "Doubleday myth" is as entertaining as a day at the ballpark.

Abner Doubleday

The Search for Baseball's Origins

The story of the Doubleday myth begins with Albert Goodwill Spalding. Spalding was a baseball pitcher. In 1871, he joined the Boston Red Stockings of the National Association, the first **professional** baseball **league**. The National Association became the National League (NL) in 1876. Spalding ended his playing days in 1877. He later became owner of the Chicago White Stockings.

Albert Spalding

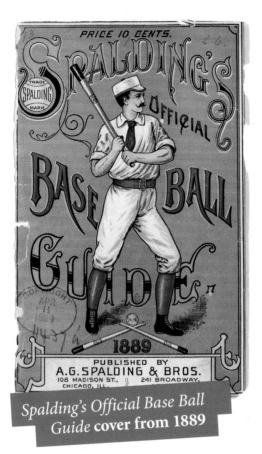

Spalding opened a sporting goods store in Chicago. He then set up a company that made the balls used by the National League. Spalding also wrote *Spalding's Official Base Ball Guide*. It contained the records of players and teams and stories about baseball history. The book was published every year and was the most popular book of its kind.

Spalding's Official Base Ball Guide **cover from 1889**

Henry Chadwick was the **editor** of *Spalding's Official Base Ball Guide*. Born in England, Chadwick was considered the authority on baseball.

Henry Chadwick

"America's Game?"

Spalding believed baseball could shape America. He thought the game taught the values of hard work and fair play. It had healthy **competition**. He said it was played in "an enthusiastic and American manner."

People playing a game of rounders in 1913

A baseball game in 1860

By 1900, a wave of **nationalism** was sweeping the country. The nation had come together following the Civil War. The United States was becoming a world power. U.S. pride soared. Americans wanted a sport they could call their own.

In the 1903 edition of Spalding's guide, Henry Chadwick wrote that baseball came from the English game of rounders. Chadwick's words made Spalding want to prove that baseball was an American creation.

Fact!

To promote baseball as America's game, Spalding led teams of U.S. baseball players on a world tour in 1888–1889. The teams played against each other in Australia and countries in Europe and the Middle East.

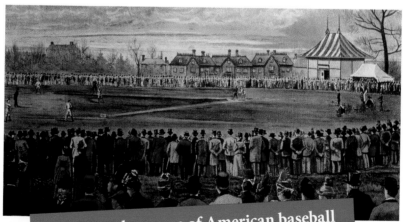

People watch a game of American baseball stars in London, England, in 1889.

A Search for the Truth

Baseball and rounders have some similarities but are different in many ways. Chadwick had played rounders as a child in England in the late 1820s and early 1830s, before even hearing about baseball. Because the games were similar, he assumed rounders was older than baseball.

Spalding was outraged: How could his own editor claim the American game originated in a foreign country? He had to show that baseball had been born on American soil.

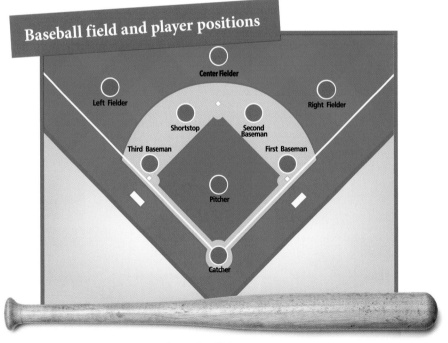

baseball bat

In 1905, Spalding created a **commission** to study baseball's origin. The Mills Commission was made up of old friends who generally shared Spalding's opinion. The men included **politicians** and former baseball players. Through articles in newspapers, the group asked all Americans who knew anything about baseball's roots to come forward.

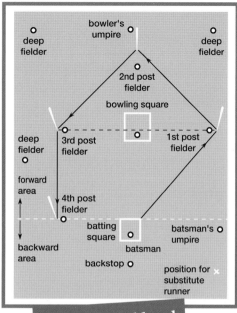

Rounders field and player positions

rounders bat

Chapter Two

Enter Abner Graves

Spalding's efforts sparked national interest. The commission received many responses. Most of the letters came from elderly people who recalled playing many types of bat-and-ball games.

Abner Graves of Denver, Colorado, Tells How the Present National Game Had Its Origin.

Abner C. Graves, mining engineer of Denver, Col., claims to know all about the origin of the game of base ball. He is stopping at the Thuma hotel, and reading the article in Saturday's Beacon Journal from the pen of A. C. Spalding prepared the following article and submitted it to the Beacon Journal for publication:

"I notice in Saturday's Beacon Journal a question as to origin of base ball from the pen of A. G. Spalding, and requesting that data on the subject be sent to J. E. Sullivan, 15 Warren street, New York.

his innings the same as in "old cat." There being generally from 20 to 50 boys in the field, collisions often occurred in the attempt of several to catch the ball. Abner Doubleday then figured out and made a plan of improvement on town ball to limit the number of players, and have equal sides, calling it 'base ball' because it had four bases, three being where the runner could rest free of being put out by keeping his foot on the flat stone base, while next one on his side took the bat, the first runner be-

Then things got interesting. In April 1905, the editors of *The Akron Beacon Journal*, a newspaper in Ohio, received a curious letter. The letter was from a 71-year-old man named Abner Graves. Graves was responding to an article written by Spalding.

The article asked for information about baseball's beginnings. Graves also sent a copy of his letter to Spalding's commission.

In his letter, Graves claimed that as a young boy he had heard about the birth of baseball while living in Cooperstown, New York.

Cooperstown, New York, 1800s

Letters that Shaped Baseball History

Graves reported that Abner Doubleday was on a Cooperstown ball field in 1838 or 1839. At that time, Doubleday had drawn a diagram of the first baseball field for the kids playing there.

Spalding was overjoyed when he heard about Graves's letter. After all, Abner Doubleday was a hero of the Civil War. He had been a general in the U.S. Army and had won honors at the Battle of Gettysburg.

Spalding asked Graves for more details. In his second letter, Graves changed his story. He claimed he had actually played in the game and that he was in college at the time. Graves also included a diagram he drew that supposedly matched Doubleday's.

Fact!

Doubleday grew up in Auburn, New York. As a young man, he studied at a military school in Cooperstown, about 100 miles (161 kilometers) away.

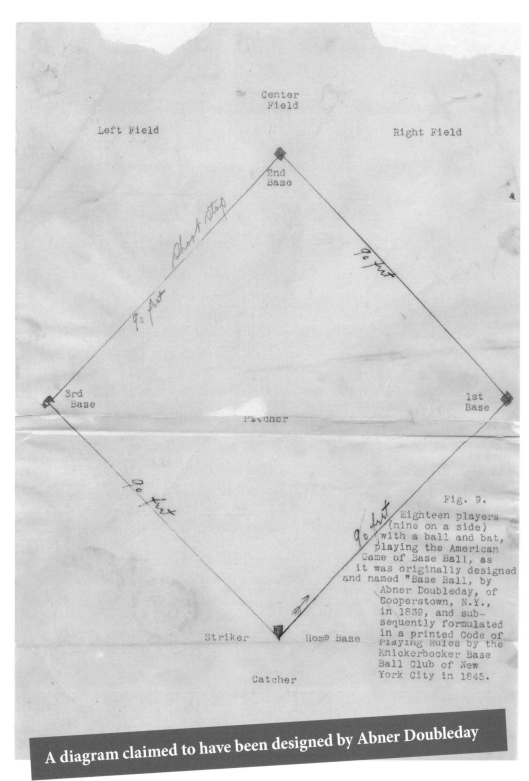

Center
Field

Left Field

Right Field

2nd
Base

Short Stop

go first

go first

3rd
Base

1st
Base

Pitcher

Fig. 9.

Eighteen players
(nine on a side)
with a ball and bat,
playing the American
Game of Base Ball, as
it was originally designed
and named "Base Ball, by
Abner Doubleday, of
Cooperstown, N.Y.,
in 1839, and sub-
sequently formulated
in a printed Code of
Playing Rules by the
Knickerbocker Base
Ball Club of New
York City in 1845.

go first

go out

Striker

Home Base

Catcher

A diagram claimed to have been designed by Abner Doubleday

15

Spalding's "Proof"

Graves's claims were impossible to prove. But that didn't matter to Spalding. He believed he now had proof that baseball was an American invention.

The commission's report was published in *Spalding's Official Base Ball Guide* in 1908. It concluded that Abner Doubleday did indeed invent baseball in 1839 in Cooperstown. The report, however, changed some of the details in Graves's letters. The changes were made to fit with the rules of baseball as it was played at the time.

Armed with what he felt was **evidence**, Spalding excitedly spread the news. In his book, *America's National Game*, Spalding tapped into the country's strong sense of nationalism. He praised baseball as the symbol of "American Courage, Confidence . . . American Energy, Eagerness, Enthusiasm. . . ."

Artist's sketch of Uncle Sam holding a baseball bat for the cover of Spalding's book

The Myth Is Born

Spalding sold thousands of copies of the book to libraries and men's organizations. The Doubleday myth began appearing in schoolbooks and encyclopedias. Newspapers were quick to run with the story as well. The Cooperstown tale spread like wildfire. Americans were quick to believe baseball was their homegrown invention. But were Graves's claims true? Many people challenged Graves's story.

Doubleday died in 1893, so he wasn't alive to weigh in on the debate. But in 1839, Doubleday had attended the U.S. Military Academy at West Point, about 150 miles (241 km) south of Cooperstown.

Abner Doubleday

Historians could not find any connection between Doubleday and baseball in any of his letters or diaries. Doubters also questioned why Graves had changed important details of his story.

The U.S. Military Academy at West Point

A MAN'S GAME?

Spalding claimed that baseball was not a sport to be played by women. "Base Ball is too strenuous for womankind, except as she may take part in the grandstand with applause for brilliant play," he wrote. To him, the American game had to be rugged and manly. Female

Eri Yoshida

players such as Mamie Johnson, Eri Yoshida, and Doris Sams proved Spalding wrong. Today, women's teams and leagues exist around the world.

Chapter Three

A New Challenge

Despite the doubters, most Americans accepted the Cooperstown story. Based on Graves's letters, the Mills Commission had declared baseball was born in 1839. By the 1930s, the sport began gearing up for a celebration of its 100th anniversary.

People in a parade walk down Main Street on the way to Doubleday Field on opening day of the Baseball Hall of Fame.

During this time, Cooperstown officials wanted to increase tourism in their village. They decided to build a museum in the town to honor Doubleday and the so-called birthplace of baseball. A wealthy Cooperstown landowner gave money and a plot of land to build the museum.

The museum gathered documents, photos, and literature related to baseball. The items also included bats, baseballs, and old scorecards. The Baseball Hall of Fame opened on June 12, 1939.

Inside the Baseball Hall of Fame in Cooperstown, New York

Ignoring the Facts

Meanwhile, a librarian in New York City named Robert W. Henderson was researching baseball's true origins. In April 1939, his work was published in the *Bulletin of the New York Public Library*. Relying on old books and newspapers, Henderson proved that the Doubleday story was not true.

Henderson's evidence included a diagram of baseball's familiar diamond-shaped infield printed in the mid-1830s. He also showed that similar rules in baseball had been published in 1828 for the game rounders. Henderson's findings were widely reported.

But the museum opening was only weeks away. Cooperstown and Major League Baseball decided to ignore Henderson's work. "No one was willing to let it rain on Cooperstown's parade," wrote journalist Brian Martin.

Today, almost 300,000 people visit the Baseball Hall of Fame and Museum each year.

BASEBALL IN JAPAN

Baseball is Japan's most popular sport. Horace Wilson, an American-born teacher at a Japanese university, introduced the sport to Japan in the early 1870s. Today, small differences exist between American and Japanese baseball. The ball used in Japanese games is bigger and harder than the American ball. Unlike the American game, Japanese games can end in a tie.

The True Origins

The grand celebration in Cooperstown went on as planned. Baseball celebrated its birthday, and the new museum opened. In a letter, President Franklin Delano Roosevelt praised Doubleday for inventing "the great American sport." The Cooperstown story remained in the history books.

Meanwhile, others continued to explore the origins of baseball. Their work has shown that the sport **evolved** from simple bat-and-ball games, including rounders. These children's games were brought to the American colonies by English settlers.

Crowds celebrate the 100-year anniversary of the birth of baseball in Cooperstown.

Como igaua a pelota os mancebos en vn prado. —

Como o ronzel casou con outra moller 1leyrou santa maria

Over time, these children's games were modified into baseball. Documents show that forms of the game were played in the 1700s in New York, Philadelphia, and Massachusetts.

One thing is certain: Neither Abner Doubleday, nor any other single person, invented America's pastime.

Does It Matter?

Some Americans are still unwilling to accept the truth of baseball's origins. In October 2010, then Commissioner of Baseball Bud Selig wrote, "I really believe that Abner Doubleday is the 'Father of Baseball.' I know there are some historians who would dispute this though." Researchers and historians made fun of the commissioner's comments. They questioned why the head of baseball would support the false Cooperstown legend.

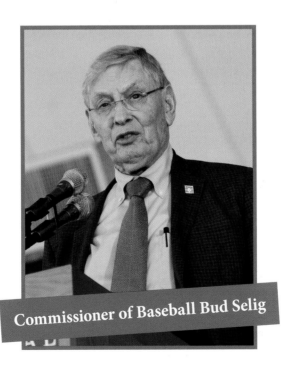

Commissioner of Baseball Bud Selig

Abner Doubleday

Yet, like a good mystery novel, the Doubleday story fascinates baseball fans. Why did Graves write the letters? Had his memories faded since watching or playing baseball in Cooperstown? If he made up the story, why? Was he seeking attention?

Research has shown that the Doubleday story is a myth—and a powerful one at that. The tale created by an old man shaped not only the game but also the United States. The enduring legend has captured the hearts of generations of Americans—just like the game of baseball itself.

A modern-day baseball game between the LA Dodgers and the Arizona Diamondbacks

Fact vs. Fiction
Did Abner Doubleday Invent Baseball?

Fiction

Abner Doubleday, a Civil War general, invented baseball in Cooperstown, NY, in 1839.

Fact

Abner Doubleday did not invent baseball. In 1839, Doubleday was a student at the U.S. Military Academy at West Point.

There is no mention of Doubleday's connection to baseball found in any of his letters or diaries.

The modern game of baseball evolved from various ball-and-stick games that were brought to the American colonies by British settlers in the 1700s.

Fiction

Abner Graves, a mining engineer, witnessed the first game of baseball as a young boy in Cooperstown in 1839.

Fact

Abner Graves probably saw baseball played in Cooperstown as a young boy. A form of the sport, however, had been played in the United States since the 1700s. Graves may even have played baseball in Cooperstown, but he did not play in the sport's first game, as he claimed in his second letter.

Glossary

commission (kuh-MISH-uhn)—a group of people who meet to solve a particular problem

competition (kahm-puh-TISH-uhn)—a contest of some kind

editor (ED-ih-tur)—the person who is in charge of a newspaper or a magazine

evidence (EV-ih-duhns)—information and facts that help prove something is true or not true

evolve (ih-VAHLV)—to develop and change as a result of many small steps

league (LEEG)—a group of teams that compete against each other in a specific sport

modification (mod-ih-fih-KAY-shun)—a slight change in something to meet a specific need

nationalism (NASH-uh-nuh-lism)—an extreme form of patriotic feeling

politician (pol-uh-TISH-uhn)—someone who runs for or holds a government office

professional (pruh-FESH-uh-nuhl)—making money for doing something others do as a hobby or an activity

Read More

Jacobs, Greg. *The Everything Kids' Baseball Book: From Baseball History to Today's Favorite Players*. Avon, MA: Adams Media, 2020.

MacKinnon, Adam C. *Baseball for Kids: A Young Fan's Guide to the History of the Game*. Emeryville, CA: Rockridge Press, 2020.

Panchyk, Richard. *Baseball History for Kids: America at Bat from 1900 to Today*. Chicago: Chicago Review Press, 2016.

Internet Sites

Baseball Facts and Worksheets
kidskonnect.com/sports/baseball/

Baseball History, American History and You
baseballhall.org/baseball-history-american-history-and-you

History of baseball in the United States
kids.kiddle.co/History_of_baseball_in_the_United_States

Index